AF259501

**To** ___________________________

**From** _________________________

all you
NEED IS
Love

Love
is all
Around

with you
FOREVER

all you
NEED IS
Love

hugs
AND
KISSES

Love

all you
NEED IS
Love

Love
is all
Around

hugs
AND
KISSES

with you
FOREVER

Love

you are
so
loved

all you
NEED IS
Love

Love
is all
Around

hugs
AND
KISSES

with you
FOREVER

I ♥ U

you are
so
loved

all you
NEED IS
Love

Love
is all
Around

with you
FOREVER

all you
NEED IS
Love

hugs
AND
KISSES

all you
NEED IS
Love

Love
is all
Around

with you
FOREVER

you are
so
loved

all you
NEED IS
Love

Love
is all
Around

hugs
AND
KISSES

with you
FOREVER

Love

you are
so
loved

all you
NEED IS
Love

Love
is all
Around

with you
FOREVER

I ♥ U

Love

you are
so
loved

all you
NEED IS
Love

Love
is all
Around

with you
FOREVER

Love

you are
so
loved

all you
NEED IS
Love

Love
is all
Around

I ♥ U

all you
NEED IS
Love

Love
is all
Around

Copyright © 2020 Love Notes Press

All Rights Reserved

No part of this publication maybe reproduced, distributed, or transmitted in any form or by any means, including photocopying, recording, or other electronic or mechanical methods, without the prior written permission of the publisher, Love Notes Press.

Time to head back to
Amazon to order
another book. If you
enjoyed this notebook,
we hope you will
share your opinion
by leaving a review
on Amazon.
Thank you,
Love Notes Press

www.ingramcontent.com/pod-product-compliance
Lightning Source LLC
Chambersburg PA
CBHW051813050726
47598CB00006B/2545